Revolutionary Economics:
Amending the Market System to Incentivize Efficiency
First Edition

By: John James Delaney III

Revolutionary Economics:
Amending the Market System to Incentivize Efficiency

Abstract: This essay proposes changes to the current economic system by attempting to manipulate the economic incentives around the constraints which have been most burdensome to market economies in operating efficiently. To do this, I propose a three step system that will influence the allocation of resources or the incentives of production. This essay assumes that the natural and recurring constraints to the market system *can be* modified so as to increase the level of efficient production in market economies. The first part seeks to resolve the main problem (polarization of money, which leads to recessions) facing market economies voluntarily by creating new incentives for persons to invest in government bonds; the second identifies that taxes can be specialized based on a ratio of income and expenditures and the rate of growth rather than total income; the last part regarding monetary policy will be used to effect outstanding and inefficient market powers (such as a welfare state or a monopoly economy) that fail to be resolved by the first two proposals.

Introduction

The future is unpredictable. Economics as a study is often attacked for its inability to deduce models which consistently describe the state of affairs in the economy, and in particular, which policy recommendation is most effective in improving the general state of affairs. Politically, the difficulties are even more dramatic. For every policy proposal, objections are also proposed: for example, in response to the 2008 crisis, expansionary fiscal policy was implemented, but there is still endless contempt both in the field of economics and politics criticizing the increased federal spending.

An analysis attempting to determine the most effective school of thought (monetarism, classical, new classical, Keynesian, new Keynesian, Austrian, and other forms of heterodox market economics) is not the point of this essay: rather, I will propose amendments to our current market system, amendments which hope to increase the efficiency in the areas of the economy most dramatically in need of revision.

I am of the opinion that the world economy is capable of experiencing a surge in efficiency and growth, and I am altogether not opposed to the idea that this surge in growth shall last indefinitely. Although there may never be such a thing as utopia, history has shown that even the most implausible ends can be achieved (take for example the case of controlled electricity, satellites, and the internet; all of which would be considered impossible feats by those of the distant to not so distant past). The study of economics has a common purpose of *continually increasing efficiency,* and this purpose will continue to be sought by those in business and those who study economics. Efficiency, it may be helpful to explain, can be understood as a general betterment of society; to give definition, we may assume the utilitarian creed: what is best for society would be the actions/events which tend to maximize the pleasure (or profit) of society, or likewise, to minimize the pains (or costs) of that society on the aggregate.

      This ideal conception of efficiency is met with certain restraints: it is such that the feudal system, although minor alterations may have been made by certain agents to increase the efficiency of the system in small ways up until its destruction, the feudal system itself was incapable of increasing efficiency beyond a limited end. Many economists have considered capitalism void of such restraints, they believe that the forces of the market system will continue to increase in efficiency (it is simply the nature of the market system!); I am personally of the opinion that this is undoubtedly correct and that gains of efficiency are made every minute of the day by rational agents (rational in the general economic sense), the culmination of which can be best seen after long periods of time (usually accompanied with many different zcases of creative destruction). If we maintain this theory, it is evident that the market system will never be replaced by some derivation of a command economy unless such an economy can be shown to be more efficient over longer periods of time. Such a result has already taken place to a certain extent, specifically, Keynesian economics. That is, the role of government *does* have an essential role in maintaining the existence of the market system; this being the case, it is not the case that government intervention *replaces* the market system, it simply helps it perform better.

In the following essay, the first section is devoted to voluntary redistribution; that is, I propose amendments to the bond market to increase the incentive of investing in it so that the income earned from bonds will reduce the amount of money which must be taken coercively by taxation. This is as laissez faire as we get throughout the model; the assumption is that by reducing taxes, the market system can work at its highest level of effective demand without government intervention. It should also be evident after reading the first section that the model incentivizes a large private sector in comparison to a large public sector, for two reasons in particular: 1) the majority of people will have to pay high (relative) taxes if the deficit cannot be made up via bonds, thus by democratic vote, the rational person will seek to minimize the level of government spending; and 2) 'elitists', who are those most likely to invest given the high price of bonds and who may also be said to greatly influence our politics, will resist the circumstance of the deficit in relation to GDP increasing past the point of when they bought into the market; this is because bond rates will increase as the deficit increases in relation to GDP (as we will propose later) and as interest rates increase, bonds with lower interest rates will decrease in value.

In the second section, I propose a mathematical model for an equilibrium tax rate. Higher positive values symbolize a higher tax rate whereas negative values symbolize a government subsidy. The ratio will increase as the average propensity to save increases for the person in question as well as in the aggregate and also as the rate of growth decreases. Likewise, the tax rate will decrease as expenditures increase in relation to income in each person as well as in the aggregate and as income grows from one year to the next. What is the purpose for this? First, both households and firms should be incentivized to increase their income (wages and employment) from one year to the next, symbolizing *growth*. Second, gluts are caused when there exists a shortage of demand; shortages of demand are most often caused by the existence of severe wealth inequality. For example, in the 'paradox of poverty amidst potential plenty' we see that as countries grow more affluent, their marginal propensity to consume tends to decrease. As Keynes has pointed out, the lower the MPC and the greater the MPS, the more difficult it becomes for the private sector to translate all the money stored in savings into investment; this creates recessions, in which case the government, acting dutifully, must step in to correct. It is my understanding that if all people were incentivised to spend a relatively reasonable portion of their income, then the private sector could operate independent of government intervention even as wealth increases. Thirdly, by incentivising all forms of expenditure by firms and households alike, the demand for both consumption and investment will rise; the increase in consumption offsetting the costs of investment. The increase in real investment will lead to a greater standard of living generally. Fourthly, as the propensity to consume increases within the aggregate, the tax rate for each individual should decrease to reflect the decreased need for government intervention since the private sector is more capable of maintaining itself.

It is often argued that there will come a time where the rate of growth (or in the terms stated beforehand, *the ability for the economy to increase in efficiency*) will reach a certain limit where an *increase* in the rate of growth becomes impossible, and instead the growth rate will stabilize around some relatively small rate of growth indefinitely. Intuitively, given our current system and knowledge of economics, this is clearly the case. Human nature however, has a different expectation: it is likely (to myself and many) that human nature will continue to seek to better itself, it is also the likelihood of human nature that some people will seek different levels of pleasure (or profit) in comparison to others. At such a point in time in which growth rates were to stabilize, there is no reason why such economic stabilization will translate into a stabilization in human nature: human wants and desires will continue to be limitless in scope, and it is likely that the utility expectations of certain persons will be greater than the low rate of growth will allow. In such a circumstance, human nature is likely to prevail as always, and certain agents will still fulfill their expectations if not by altering the economic system to one which would scaffold their success then by capitalizing on the ignorance/weakness of others by engaging in ridiculous lawsuits, or by "cutting corners" and breaking the law to fulfill their endless desire for happiness. Overcoming this claim is a further goal of this essay and economics in general.

From this it is evident that even in a society which has been productive enough to squander any further gains from production, the desires of people will exceed the ability for such persons to fulfill their expectations.

Are we then resolved that even in the most utopian societies, there will still be material wants and desires that will go unfulfilled? Maybe, maybe not. If society has reached a point in its level of technology that all wants/desires can be fulfilled, then there is nothing to worry about; if on the other hand, people are left unsatisfied, then it is likely (if it is possible) for things to become more corrupt at the cost of satisfaction of society as a whole .

The following essay, I like to think, is the first of its kind. My objective, plainly stated, is to characterize an economic system which is capable of maneuvering around the constraints which pose a threat to the ability to increase efficiency. To this purpose, I had begun my contemplation over a year ago asking the question: What would be the ideal economic system? On a whim, I decided to address distributive justice, identifying that the main factor inhibiting such an ideal system is an inefficient allocation of resources (severe wealth inequality). That is, if modifications were to be made in the way that resources were allocated, then potentially such an ideal system could arise. The evidence for this belief lies in the fact that there is a great, unused storage of wealth owned by the most affluent which does little to benefit them any further but would, if reallocated, make a major contribution to the lower classes (this is commonly known as diminishing marginal utility). This being possible, would it then be just? The simple answer is no. Just because we can achieve a situation where all would be shared so that the 'greatest summation of happiness' is maximized, this ideal cannot stand alone: that is, there is nothing which suggests that such an allocation would be cyclic in practice; in other words, it would not be a self maintaining *system* (as clearly shown by communism). How then, is such distributive justice possible? Without further ado, the following is the contents of my proposed amendment to the current market system.

Part I
Voluntary reallocation as the ideal form of reallocation

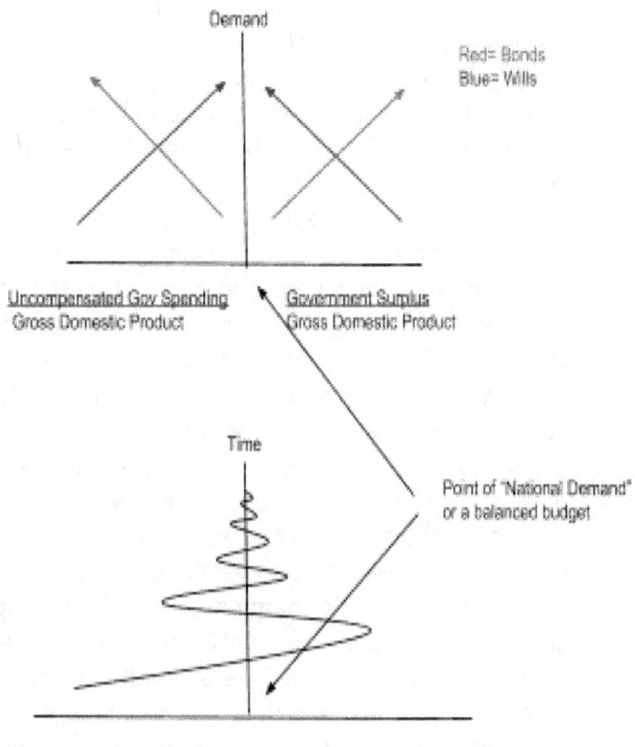

In this first section I propose amendments to the current bond market (changes which will not meet its full potential until they are also adopted by foreign nations). The analysis will go as follows: 1) artificially determining the interest rate of bonds so that there is a supply of bonds which will be purchased to offset the national demand for bonds (national demand is that money value necessary to balance the federal budget; if this amount is achieved entirely by the sale of bonds, taxation would not be necessary, and therefore prohibited). The interest rate must rise in proportion as the level of government deficit rises in comparison to gross GDP. More specifically, the interest rate of a standard bond will be exactly equal to the ratio ((Government spending - Income from bonds)/(GDP)). The length of a standard bond shall be twelve years. a 6 year bond, being one half the time period, will receive one half the interest rate which would be offered to those who buy a 12 year bond. For example: if the government deficit is $40,000 and GDP is $100,000 then the ratio set forth will equal 40%; if a person were to buy a 12 year bond at this time, their interest rate of return would be the initial bond amount plus 40% that amount. If the same macroeconomic conditions hold, but the person were to buy a 1.2 year length bond instead, the interest rate would be 4% instead of 40% because a 1.2 year bond is one tenth that of a 12 year bond. This relationship between deficit/GDP and interest rate, shown graphically, would be a demand curve which rises in proportion to government deficit.

2) Assuming the first amendment fails to attract enough speculation to offset national demand, a new addition to the bond market will be instituted (simultaneously) to increase speculative demand in the

bond market: this new addition will be termed "Land Wills" (because the holder of the 'Will' will earn a share of income from those who visit or immigrate to the land which the investor helps to maintain) or just simply "Wills". This term gets its name from the fact that this new addition will not be transferable on the market but only upon death of the will holder; this point is extremely important: the supply of bonds with wills attached must be sold on a highly controlled auction market. There are two reasons for this: 1) the money price paid in purchasing a bond/will should be as high as possible if there is to be a hope of offsetting the national demand; and 2) to keep the number of wills in the hands of the people as low as possible (so that the dividends paid to will holders are significant and add to the incentive for purchasing wills, this point will be introduced next). The source of income for wills will come from those who pay the necessary fee to enter the economy/country. For example, if somebody wants to immigrate to the United States, they will be required to pay a certain fee (which, upon adoption from other countries, will be determined primarily by market forces instead of by congress) the money value of which will be equally distributed to the will holders (much like stock dividends) and not paid directly to the federal government (this point is essential for reasons of incentive). In graphical terms, demand will rise as the deficit falls due to an increase in government income obtained by selling government bonds; this is because as the deficit falls due to increased speculation in the bond/will market, tax rates as a percentage of income falls for every tax bracket (this fall in taxes is the preferred reallocation I speak of), increasing the tax free income of the majority of persons under which the government governs. This increase in income will inspire more immigration demand (and many other types of demand as well), which will likewise increase the nominal value of the dividends to will holders; this rise in immigration demand will symbolize a greater flow of money to the owners of wills, which will then be met with greater speculative demand as the ratio of uncompensated spending/ GDP nears the equilibrium range. 3) Income earned from wills will be dispersed regularly, unlike bonds. Also, the length of time which a person (or family) can own and earn income on a will is indefinite, unlike the fixed amount of time which bonds take to mature. Most importantly, the bond cannot be cashed unless upon sacrifice of owning the will. This last point deserves some clarification: upon purchasing a will/bond; the owner will essentially be buying a will backed by a bond: if a will/bond is bought for $100,000, then the owner may continue to receive his/her proportion of income earned from immigration past the point of bond maturity (both in figures of money value as well as time length), but in doing so, they do not collect the $100,000 plus interest even if the bond has matured insofar as the owner continues to receive his/her share of income from immigrating persons. If a person values the will greater than the bond then the due payment of the matured bond may be postponed indefinitely.

4) The market for wills/bonds must be maintained as an auction market past the point of national demand. People must always be allowed to invest in the proposed market, and this factor is essential if the market is to be maintained (as will be illustrated later). As the interest rate rises past national demand, and a greater government surplus is achieved, the interest rate begins to rise (instead of falling as more money enters the market) proportionately as the ratio (surplus/GDP) rises. The interest rate will then be equal

to (surplus/GDP) for a 12 year bond and respectively less for bonds of shorter duration.

Further, when in the surplus range, to prevent a significant loss in money circulation (and to likewise prevent excessive government spending), the amount received in the bond/will market shall be put to clear the economy of student loan debt.

5) To ensure national security, only citizens of the United States may invest into the market unless in the equilibrium range. This range should be where the (deficit/GDP) measure equals 10% through the point of national demand and up until the point of 10% in the (surplus/GDP) measure.

How the system works

Initially, assuming there is a high deficit; when the market opens, the interest rates which can be obtainable by purchasing government bonds is capable of exceeding interest rates offered by banks (depending on the chosen time it takes for the bond to mature (this time period will be offered in 10 year increments and must be chosen immediately after the auction has been won)). These high relative interest rates will transfer a great deal of speculative demand out of the private sector markets, this is not a bad thing (and rather a good thing) because it will eliminate the possibility of artificial bubbles in the stock market: this relationship is drawn because in order for speculative demand to shift, the reason for changing markets or stocks will be solely because the rate of return in the new market/stock is higher, not because the new investment option offers any greater value in real terms. As speculative investment in the will/bond market grows, the deficit decreases, decreasing the tax rate in proportion to income for every tax bracket, increasing immigration demand and likewise speculative demand for wills in particular (since as the deficit level decreases, the interest rate also decreases, lowering demand for bonds but increasing the demand for wills because of the increase in immigration inspired by the lower average tax rate). This will continue to the equilibrium range, at which point US Citizens will have to compete with agents in other nations in the auction market (agents in other nations, having the opportunity to, in a sense, "buy American land" (a notion derived because they will earn income off of the land by means of immigration), will likely be fierce competitors and take the market throughout this range). As the level of income increases up to and past the point of national demand, taxes are abolished! As money pours into the hands of our government, we reach the surplus range, as the surplus grows, the interest rate for bonds grows once again, leading to a new spike in demand for the bond/will market. This cannot continue forever due to demand causing such a large increase in the number of wills preventing any significant income from being earned from the immigration side of the market (again, lowering demand for wills as the federal budget becomes further from the equilibrium rate). At which point, people will be inclined to forgo the income earned off of the will, and will then cash in their matured bond; which will lower the surplus, and possibly create a deficit (which will be smaller than the initial deficit, assuming: 1) that there are still some agents who have yet to cash in their bonds 2) the growth in GDP throughout this period was mainly influenced by the private sector (decreasing the applicable ratio) and the government did not grow excessively during the surplus range). If these assumptions are to hold, the ratio of deficit or surplus divided by GDP will continue to near the equilibrium range rather than being forced further outward to greater deficit or surplus levels; stabilizing at the optimum point of national demand.

Part II
Finding Justice in a Coercive Taxation System

When the prior model fails to meet national demand, and the government maintains a deficit, a self supporting economy will turn to its taxpayers to compensate for such deficit.

I posit that there is an abstract measure of distributive justice that can be derived from these three variables alone. The equation is such:
(Income*Savings*aggregate APS)/(Expenditures*Growth Rate*Nominal Taxes). Before I introduce the equation in its entirety, I will introduce it in the manner I discovered it.

The 'original equation' introduces a ratio (consider as flow variables rather than stock) which asses, intuitively, a measure of wealth in relation to work, or income in relation to effort.

That is, net income minus total expenditures, put in terms of (divided by) total expenditures (this is to represent a flow measure of savings in relation to expenditures, a value which rational agents seek to maximize) in relation (divided by) to gross income minus net income put in terms of (divided by) net income (this is a flow measure of taxation in proportion to disposable income, an equation which rational agents seek to minimize); all this multiplied by the aggregate average propensity to save divided by the growth rate. My hypothesis for this section is that every legally defined person (corporations included) has an equilibrium tax rate which is equal to ((Income*Savings*Aggregate Average Propensity to save)/(Total Expenditures*Rate of Growth*Nominal Taxes)).

Irrespective of the measure of income, factors which have the biggest effect on our economy is the ratio of net income divided by total expenditures; this measure, if equal to one, is the mathematical definition of Say's law in full effect ("supply creates its own demand"). If the aggregate of this measure is greater than one (in the aggregate), then there is a leakage in demand which signifies that if this relationship were to continue over a certain indeterminate period of time, eventually there will be a recession because savings continues to grow at a rate greater than expenditures which cannot be indefinitely maintained if the economy is to continue to exist (this is because the velocity of money will slow to the point where output or prices or both must fall in accordance with the quantity theory of money $MV=PY$, money supply assumed to be static

(M=Money, V=Velocity, P=Prices, Y=Output/Income)).
To resolve this and allow for much needed savings accounts, the value greater than one obtained by the previous ratio must be offset by the ratio of savings divided by taxation, the nominal value of taxation exceeding the nominal value of savings. This is both classical economics and Keynesian economics at work! The original equation's intention is to determine the equilibrium tax rate for each individual separately, because the aggregate is only composed of individual agents.

Taxing incomes by brackets is highly unjust and inefficient. Those at the upper margin of a lower tax bracket have a lower tax rate and lose less money and make more money after taxes than those in the lower margin of the next higher tax bracket. These tax rates can be modified to be more specialized to each person; and further, the level of income alone has absolutely no significance as to whether the person (or corporation) in question does either good or bad for the economy: the point of significance is, again, the ratio between net income and total expenditures, and if this ratio is to lead to a recession in the long run, then the relationship between net income/total expenditures and savings/taxation is the most important factors in consideration when addressing the long term health of an economy.

In its simplified form, the ratio is expressed as net income multiplied by nominal savings divided by total expenditures multiplied by nominal taxes. Or

$$\frac{(I)(S)(AAPS)}{(E)(Gr)(T)}$$

Where I=income, S=savings, AAPS=aggregate average propensity to save (measure of savings in relation to income of the entire economy), E=expenditures, Gr=growth rate.

The enforcement of this tax system will take the value earned for each person at the time when taxes are due, and adjust the tax rate to the value obtained. The value obtained, whether above or below such persons income tax bracket tax rate will determine whether the individual will either be taxed more or have a tax refund respectively.

In practice, we see that as the marginal propensity to expend (expenditures being both consumption and investment) rises, the equilibrium tax rate falls; which is intuitively ideal because it signifies a stronger private sector, and less dependence on government, the closer Say's Law is to being in full effect. In the situation that all net income earned is equal to total expenditures, marginal savings equals zero and the model begets a value of zero, so the equilibrium tax rate for all persons with such income/expenditure ratios, regardless of the level of income, should be returned all the money previously taken out from taxes (because these people are fulfilling their part in maintaining a cyclical system, see Say's Law in other readings).

Allow me to now address why the rate of growth must be factored in. Although it is true what has gone before (specifically, the money held as savings, if not invested by other firms or government, signifies a *leakage* in the economy, this leakage increases, burdening our economy more and more as the amount of savings which is not invested increases), firms which are efficient should not be burdened. A firm which has a high income while also having low expenditures would have a higher tax rate than if this firm were to increase their expenditures (most likely in the form of new investment); but the firm should also be awarded if, although their investment is low, they continue to make greater and greater profits from one year to the next. This situation (of a firm with an increasing growth rate) can rightfully be considered an efficient allocation of resources, and the tax rate should decrease as the growth rate increases.

Now allow me to address why I include the aggregate average propensity to save into the model: if the economy is performing independently of government, there is no reason why any firm or person should be taxed a large amount. So, as the aggregate expends a greater portion of their income, there will be less need for government intervention, and the tax rate for all persons will decrease.

The way the model is arranged creates a difficulty in policy if costs happen to be greater than income due to borrowing. In this case, the government should *subsidize* such persons. This policy implication may be culpable to many. The fear is that the government would be incentivizing debtors. This however is not the case, often times credit is increased because people or firms decide to purchase durable goods including real capital; these purchases should not be looked at negatively, rather, they should be looked at positively, and rewarded.

A common situation where expenditures would be greater than income would be the case of starting a new business or running an old business which had a larger value for investment than a value of income. These new business often need a kick start, and businesses who partake in such large investment opportunities should be rewarded. There may arise the situation where a struggling business is subsidized, in which case the economic gains would translate into a greater level of competition and thus a higher measure of consumer surplus in that industry; such outcomes in increased efficiency would outweigh the outcome if struggling businesses were subjected to the harsh reality of the market system and failed as a result.

Now for some much needed examples: lets say a person were to make $18,000 in gross income last year, and this year they make $20,000 in gross, $18,000 in net; out of their net income, they spend $15,000 of it, let us also assume that the aggregate economy has a similar measure of savings in relationship to income. Place these values into the equation:

$$\frac{(I)(S)(AAPS)}{(E)(Gr)(T)}$$

where net income=I=$18,000, E=$15,000, so S=$3,000, Gr=11.11%, AAPS=0.167, T=$2,000

The rate of growth is determined by subtracting the new gross income by the old and dividing that figure by the old; average propensity to save is determined by dividing savings by income . Let's put the values in:

(18,000)(3,000)(0.167)

(15,000)(0.1111)(2,000)

which equals 2.7. So therefore, the equilibrium tax rate for this person should be 2.7 percent.

What is interesting about this model is that it is imparticular to the level of income; that is, so long as there is a similar distribution of the above variables, the tax rate will be the same. To show this, identify that the ratio was similar in the case that gross income= $20 income=$18, savings=$3, expenditures=$15, and taxes=$2. Again, the same value arises if gross income =$200,000 net income=$180,000, savings=$30,000, expenditures=$150,000, and taxes=$20,000. The importance of this should be clarified: taxes are involuntary and the government acquires them coercively. This is a burden to taxpayers, and typically the burden increases the richer a person gets; this is wholly unjust and disincentivises production. Since taxes are burdensome to taxpayers, taxes should be proportional only to the burden that taxpayers cause the economy. Persons burden the economy by hoarding wealth, not by making large incomes; rather, the concentration of wealth is a wholly good thing if it is recycled back into the economy by means of investment. This is accounted for in this model, to show this, let all factors remain constant besides expenditures and savings which will now total $7,500 and $10,500 respectively. Then we have the equation:

(18,000)**(10,500)**(0.167)
(7,500)(0.1111)(2,000)

their new tax rate equals 18.93% which is significantly higher than the previous value. Note that the aggregate average propensity to save has remained constant at 0.167, let us now perform an example of the average propensity to save decreasing to reflect an economy in which the aggregate has a similar savings/income ratio to 0.583.

$$\frac{(18,000)(10,500)(0.583)}{(7,500)(0.1111)(2,000)}$$

If the aggregate average propensity to save increases to be more conservative, this specific person would be taxed 66.19%.

If we were to assume that last years gross income was $15,000 instead of $18,000, all else remaining equal, it would signify a growth rate of 27.78% instead of 11.11%, therefore the tax rate would change to:

$$\frac{(18,000)(10,500)(0.583)}{(7,500)(0.278)(2,000)} = 26.42\%$$

which is a much more reasonable tax rate for those who are more industrious.

Let us now consider some possible alterations to the model. It is possible for expenditures to be greater than income or for the growth rate to be negative, if either one of these were to be the case, but not both, then the end value would be negative; in this case, we should subsidize such persons determined by their end value multiplied by their income. The reason for this should be elaborated; in some degree it is a social welfare program, in another degree it provides further incentive for businesses (especially start up businesses) to increase their investment levels and for persons to be less timid to purchase durable goods such as homes or vehicles. If it were to be the case that expenditures were greater than income *and* the growth rate is negative, the model would result in a positive number, and like the other people with positive numbers, a person in this circumstance will be taxed. The reasoning behind this is that a person (or firm) is going into debt, yet they have a negative growth rate; this is a clear example of an inefficient use of resources and should not be incentivized.

It may also be the case that a persons income has not increased or decreased from one year to the next; in the model, regardless of other variables, the value is undefined. If it is the case that a persons or firms income does not rise or fall from one year to the next, it may be assumed that this agent is already in equilibrium at their current tax rate. Therefore, the current taxation system will prevail and the model will have no impact.

A further note is that by incentivizing investment we may be able to keep the economy growing in real terms at an ever increasing rate and since investment will be incentivized, the full employment of economic resources is unlikely to arise, which will be a factor defending against inflation.

Part III
Monetary Policy as Determined by the State of the Economy

Given the equation in part II, it can be conceived of an economy in which the aggregate attempts to minimize their tax rate by increasing their expenditures in relationship to net income. If all persons in the economy were to increase their expenditures in relationship to income to either decrease their tax rate or receive a subsidy from the government; then *the money supply must be increased* if the nominal value of subsidies and government spending exceeds the nominal value of taxes. Further, since the equilibrium tax rate in part II depends highly on the rate of nominal growth, managing inflation is necessary in order to keep policy stable. Suppose every person and corporation in an economy seeks to receive a subsidy from the government at the time of taxes, the aggregate value of the ratio set forth in Part II will be negative. If this ratio equals or exceeds the value of negative one, the government should increase the money supply by 1% or greater (whatever the aggregate value is). If, on the other hand, the economy is rich in monopolies; profit maximizing monopolists will identify that their profits are maximized if they seek to maintain monopoly prices and low costs regardless of the possible increase in their tax rate. If the economy is monopoly rich to such an extent that the aggregate value of the former ratio in part II equals or exceeds the value of positive one, the money supply should be made to decrease by 1% or greater. The logic of this is as follows: monopolies have their beneficial purpose in producing their products/services, *however,* if the monopolist can maintain monopoly prices indefinitely, there will be no need to engage in increased investment (creating a leakage in demand as those profits are not put to other purposes). Decreasing the money supply will increase the **real** price of goods and services, this increase in real prices will **decrease real income,** which will require that consumers spend a greater portion of their income on essential commodities and decrease the proportion of their income spent on the conspicuous commodities that the monopolist produces. Monopolists will have no choice but to decrease their prices and increase their output. When the economy operates in the range (1,1) as determined by the model, money supply should be held constant, and the government should make up any deficit by means of borrowing.

This last part regarding monetary policy, will be extremely influential in giving 'lower class' laborers an amount of power to counteract monopoly power and market forces in the market system.

Conclusions:
The Structure of Market Economies Can be Arranged to be More Efficient

It is clear that there are certain constraints to market economies which prevent it from operating efficiently. Whether it be by making amendments to the current bond market, tax system, or monetary policy; changes *can be made* to resolve these problems. The foregoing analysis is logically sound since it identifies the major constraint facing market economies and incentivizes ways to resolve this constraint. As Keynes correctly theorized, investment is often less than savings.

The bond market should be adjusted so that interest rates increase as the level of government spending in proportion to GDP increases, and also to allow income from immigration go to those who scaffold our economy. This creates an independent system which equilibrates itself; this model should be instituted with the goal of voluntarily redistributing income so that those who speculate in financial markets can do so while aiding society.

Capitalists should be incentivized to spend, especially at times when they have low expectations: and in return, they will be benefitted by having a lower tax rate as a result of their increase in investment expenditures or the increase in growth.

Monetary policy should only be used when the state of the economy is in poor health; that is, when the aggregate is either in excessive and inefficient debt (welfare state) or when the aggregate can readily maintain inflated prices at the cost of efficiency (monopoly economy). Any adjustment to the market system should be in line with the virtues of property rights, and the preceding amendments do not sacrifice a single tenet which is required for market economies to operate.

This being said, the selfish judgement of some, may, at some points in time, come at the cost of the general good of society. This is not the failure of those few; it is a failure of us all in failing to institute a system which incentivizes economically sound behavior at all points in time. By instituting this system, market economies can operate to a greater and greater degree of efficiency while simultaneously making the dollar value rise as well as the standards of living. I am fortunate to concede that I cannot tell the future, but my fortune lies in the fact that the future may be bright if only slight changes were made to further the efficiency of the free market system.